It's a normal day, you are in your car going to or from work, perhaps running errands, or picking kids up from school. In an instant, your normal day could become a nightmare if a careless driver smashes into your car. It can happen in an instant.

Other than purchasing a home, your truck or automobile is likely the most expensive thing you own. And now its damaged. Worse yet, you may be hurt. Your injuries may prevent you from going to work. Not only are you forced to miss time, and likely income, but you may also be racking up medical bills, car rental bills and car repair bills. What if your car is a total loss but you haven't yet made all of the payments?

I wrote this book because this can happen to you; it can happen to anyone. And when it does, it can be devastating. And if you think the insurance company is going to take care of you - think again. If you think the insurance adjuster is on your side - think again. If you think the insurance adjuster is going to be fair - think again. Insurance companies make money by taking in payments, or premiums. They lose money when they pay out claims. The "friendly" insurance adjuster's job is to make sure their company makes money by paying out as little in claims as possible. Their job is not to be fair. Their job is to make their company money by paying as little as possible.

Allstate and State Farm together take in $100 billion - that's billion with a "B" - every year. And that is only two insurance companies. They make "political contributions" to state judges and to state and federal legislators. They have teams of lobbyists and together over 100,000 employees, all for just about one purpose - to make sure you get as little as possible when you make a claim.

If you think it's hard to beat the insurance companies - you are right. If you think it is impossible, it is not. But just like David was able to beat Goliath, you can beat the insurance companies. But to do so you must be smart and do everything right. Otherwise, the Goliath insurance company will squash you. Hopefully, this book will give you that edge.

Legal stuff

Although this book is written by an attorney - IT IS NOT LEGAL ADVICE. Every case is different and while this book may address broad questions, you should contact an attorney to consult with him about the specifics of your case.

If you have any questions, contact me.

Michael R. Wadler
2100 West Loop South, Suite 1100
Houston, Texas 77027

713/979-5936
wadler@hhjwlaw.com

Acknowledgements

I have intended to write this book for more than a few years and several people have been very helpful in getting me to this point. Larry Weinstein and Andrew Schneider both provided inspiration and acted as role models. My dear friend of more than thirty years, Steve Morris, provided excellent advice and motivation to get this project finished. My law partners have been wonderful colleagues. My parents have always believed in me and my two children never let me forget that I was always a hero in their eyes. And my beautiful and loving wife of almost 25 years who has put up with me all these years and who, every day, reminds me how special I am.

CHAPTER 1

Do I Have a Personal Injury Claim?

Not every automobile collision can result in a personal injury claim. Each claim must be evaluated on its own merits. In the most general terms, a personal injury claim has two parts - Liability and Damages.

Liability can generally be described as "whose fault was it" although the legal term is **negligence**. If an automobile collision is caused by the negligence of the other party, that is, if it was "their fault", then the possibility exists that you can recover damages from the at-fault party.

Unfortunately, it is not enough to simply claim that the other person is at fault or negligent. In order to have a valid claim you must be able to *prove* that the other person was negligent. In many circumstances, this is not difficult. One of the easiest situations involves a rear-end collision. If you are stopped or coming to a stop, and you are struck from the rear by another vehicle, most of the time the other person will be determined to be negligent.

But what if a collision occurs at an intersection? In such cases it often depends on what type of traffic control device controlled the intersection and more importantly, whether there are other witnesses to the collision.

If the collision occurs at an intersection where one person has a "stop" sign and the other doesn't, it is usually not difficult to prove that the person with the stop sign failed to yield the right-of-way after coming to a stop.

But what happens if the intersection has a red light and both parties claim the other ran the red light? The person who is bringing the claim has the burden of proof. The burden of proof in accident cases is by what is called *a preponderance of the evidence.* Preponderance is simply a big word meaning more than 50%. Many times, when each party claims that the other ran a red light, and there are no other witnesses, neither party can prove their case by a preponderance of the evidence. In such a case it may be difficult to bring a claim because neither party could prove their case. That doesn't mean that the wreck was your fault, it simply means that it may be difficult to prove that it was not your fault. It is equally as likely that one person ran the red light as it is that the other person ran the red light and an independent fact-finder may simply conclude that neither party proved their case.

Sometimes a client comes to me with this situation, and while I may believe them, the problem is that it is very difficult to "prove their case". If the other driver claims that they had a green light, it is not enough to simply say that they are wrong. In those circumstances it is too easy for someone to conclude they are 50% certain each side is right and neither side will be able to prove their case, since a preponderance of the evidence requires that the party prove his case by *more than 50%.* We refer to these cases as a "red light swearing match" and if there are no witnesses, it may be difficult to successfully bring that claim for my client.

While liability is an essential part of a claim, proving damages is also important. In a personal injury claim, damages are the injuries that someone suffers. While damage to your vehicle is certainly damages, unless you are also injured, you don't have a personal injury claim.

How serious must your injuries be? While I handle a range of injuries from very serious injuries that are life changing to relatively minor injuries, I will only consider making a claim for injuries if the injuries were serious enough to require medical attention. If you suffer a small scrape or your pain goes away in only a day, chances are your injuries may not justify making a claim. However, many times people involved in a collision are sore for several days, and the person would likely benefit from receiving medical treatment. I discuss the types of injuries you can expect to suffer later in this book, but if you require medical attention, chances are your injuries are serious enough to justify a personal injury claim.

Insurance

There is no question that proving liability and establishing damages are critical parts of being able to make a claim, but another issue is insurance. Does the person who caused the wreck have insurance to pay for the damages he caused? Or, if not, do you have insurance that will cover the losses?

I have a whole chapter devoted to the different types of insurances that may provide coverage for your loss, and my job as your attorney is to get you compensated for the damages you suffer. Or as I like to say - the doctors get you better; I get you money. Simply because the other driver does not have insurance does not mean there may not be insurance available, and as an attorney specializing in these claims, I know places that other people may overlook to find insurance coverage.

Nevertheless, in some cases there is no insurance to be found. And sadly, in those instances it may be difficult to present a claim. Why? Because it is too difficult to recover money from an individual, especially someone who can't afford insurance coverage.

If you are involved in a collision and the other party does not have insurance, don't give up. Give me a call. While there is no guarantee I can locate coverage, I am familiar with different types of insurance that may provide coverage and as I explain later in the book, I never charge a fee unless I recover money for you.

CHAPTER 2

What You Need to Know About Goliath (Things the Insurance Company doesn't want you to know)

Insurance companies like you to think that you "are in good hands" or that they will be there "like a good neighbor". One claims it provides "peace of mind". I wish that were the case.

I recall one client telling me that he had never had a problem with his insurance company - only to find out that he had never made a claim. I guess what he meant was that the insurance company gladly accepted his premium payments each month. And to tell the truth, I have never known it to be difficult for the insurance company to accept your premiums. The problems always arise when it's time for the insurance company to pay a claim. For some reason, it never seems to go as smoothly.

There are two things I cans count on with an insurance company. First, they will pay as little as possible to settle a claim. Second, they will wait as long as possible to pay the claim.

1. The insurance company will pay as little as possible

Insurance companies are ENORMOUS. The largest insurance companies are worth hundreds of billions of dollars are some of the largest companies in the world. Their business model is pretty simple. They take in more in premiums than they pay out in claims.

When they sell an insurance policy for a year, they have a pretty good idea what their revenue will be. What they don't know is how many claims will be presented. Because of this, when any one claim is presented, the insurance company makes certain that they pay as little as possible to settle that claim. It's a pretty simple formula. The less they pay in claims, the more they make in profits.

Settling an insurance claim is unlike any other type of business transaction. When you go to purchase a car, the car dealer wants to make as large a profit as possible. However, if the auto dealer tries to make too much profit, and doesn't deal with you fairly, you will simply go to another dealer or choose to buy a different type of car.

When you are trying to settle an insurance claim, the insurance company also wants to make as much profit as possible. But the way that they make profit is to pay you as little as possible. The difference between dealing with the auto dealer and the insurance company is that if the insurance company is not dealing with you fairly, you aren't free to go somewhere else.

You are stuck dealing with the insurance company that has the claim.

Insurance companies don't have to deal with you fairly. They can strong arm you all they want and there is little you can do.

Clients often tell me that they only want what is fair and that they only that to which they are entitled. Rest assured that the insurance companies have rooms of adjusters, accountants, managers, lawyers and other sorts of bean counters doing everything possible to make sure you never get one dime more than you are entitled to. In fact, unless you are willing to stand toe-to-toe with the insurance company, they will never pay you what you are entitled to. Why should they? The less they pay you, the more they can make in profit.

The one place where they can't play their games is in the court room. There, and only there, will they be called upon to pay. Unfortunately, it is only the threat of facing the judgment of twelve jurors which keeps the insurance companies "honest".

2. The insurance company will delay as long as possible

Time is on the side of the insurance company. They may know that they owe money on day one; but they are much larger than the person making the claim. They know that the longer they can delay paying a claim the greater their advantage. They can wait you out.

When your car is damaged in a collision, your car payments don't stop. Your finance company wants its money. The longer you are without a car, the harder your life becomes, and the insurance company uses that fact to its advantage to try and lower its offers.

When you are injured in an accident, you will have medical bills to pay. You may lose time from work and miss wages. All of this adds more and more pressure on you to try and resolve your claim to pay bills - some for medical expenses, others because you had to miss work because of injuries.

Insurance companies use this reality to their advantage to try and deprive you of a just and fair settlement.

The only way to level the playing field is to have an aggressive lawyer, like me, who is willing to go to bat for you and take on the insurance giant. If the insurance company knows that you have an attorney who is not afraid to take a case to a jury, they will start to negotiate in good faith to resolve your case.

3. Insurance Companies Don't Trust You

When an insurance company is presented a claim, their first thought seems to be that you are trying to commit insurance fraud. At least that's how it seems they are always approaching a claim. The adjuster will try to discredit you and find any way to get out of paying a claim.

If possible, they will try to put part of the blame for the accident on you. They will always believe their insured and try to discredit your version of the accident.

When you try to get paid for your vehicle, they will begin to lowball you and offer as little as possible. They may try to get the vehicle repaired at "their" body shop. They will make you feel as though you are trying to take advantage, when the truth is that you have been the victim of someone else's carelessness and all you want, the only thing you want, is what you are entitled to recover.

If you claim you are injured as a result of their insured's recklessness, the insurance company only becomes more suspicious. Expect them to first claim that you were not really injured. Then they will make it seem as though you are exaggerating about your injuries. Finally, they will try to claim that you were injured before.

Regardless of how they try to couch it, their argument boils down to one thing - the insurance company doesn't believe you; they think you are lying.

If your injuries are serious, they may even have you followed and spy on you to try and discredit you. Insurance companies have actually videotaped people without their knowledge, simply as a way to try and discredit the injured person.

Regardless of the commercials insurance companies run - they are not your friend. They are your adversary. And the bottom line is that you will not be treated fairly.

They will delay paying your claim, and when they finally agree to any payment it will likely be less than you deserve. They will claim you are not injured, or if you were injured that your injury is not the result of their client's negligence but is a preexisting condition. And then they will claim that your medical treatment was excessive or that the charges were too high.

At the end of the day, the only thing you can count on with the insurance company is that they will not treat you fairly.

4.   You don't have to give them a statement

The insurance company for the other driver may contact you and claim that they will not pay for the damages caused by their driver unless you give them a statement. Be careful. Many times an insurance company is trying to get a statement from you only to use it against you at a later date. The statement you make today can be used against you later.

Often I have become involved in representing a client after he has given a statement to the insurance company, and they have pried information from my client which they had no business asking, or which when taken out of context can be made to make my client appear as if he did something wrong.

If the other driver admits that she was at fault in causing the collision, there is no reason why they need to go further to investigate who caused the wreck. The only reason why they need your statement is to try to help them pay less money than they actually owe.

I believe that no one should speak with an insurance company before he speaks with an attorney.

5.   The insurance company does not have to be fair

If you purchase insurance and later make a claim, there is an obligation that the insurance company deal with you "in good faith". For example, if you have home owner's insurance and your house sustains a loss, if the insurance company does not fairly assess the loss you may have a separate claim against them. However, when you are involved in a collision with another vehicle and the ***other*** insurance contacts you, there is no duty of good faith.

Why not? Because the duty of good faith only exists with the insurance that *you purchased.* Just like the other driver may try to get out of the claim for as little as possible, his insurance company will do the same thing. The insurance company for the other driver can use every tactic, fair or unfair, in dealing with you.

For example, one insurance company refuses to pay tax, title and license fees when settling property loss. Imagine a hypothetical circumstance where someone has just purchased a brand new car for $20,000. In addition to the purchase price, he has paid tax, title and license fees, so his total cost, out the door, is $21,500. He is about to leave the dealership for the first time and someone smashes into the car and totals it. This insurance company will only pay $20,000, and will refuse to pay the additional amount for tax, title and license even though you will be unable to replace your car for $20,000.

That's not fair, but they couldn't care less.

Some insurance companies will refuse to pay for original manufactured parts when repairing your vehicle and instead will only consider the cost of off-brand parts.

That doesn't seem fair, either, but they couldn't care less.

Some insurance companies limit the amount they will pay for a rental car, regardless of the type of vehicle you have. The way I see it, if you are driving an expensive car that someone damages because he is careless, he should provide you the same type of car that he damaged while yours is being repaired. After all, that's the car that you are making payments for.

If you are making payments on a Mercedes Benz, and it gets wrecked and takes a month to repair, the insurance company might try to give you a Honda Civic to drive and consider that fair. And if you don't object, they will gladly give you a lesser value car to drive while yours is being repaired. Why? Because they don't have to be fair.

So here is a secret. The insurance company has to provide you the same type of vehicle you were driving but can't use. They won't tell you that. And unless you have a lawyer willing to fight for you, you probably won't get that.

CHAPTER 4

What about property damage?

Almost every collision involves property damage to your vehicle. In fact, most insurance companies assign one insurance adjuster to handle property damage and a different adjuster to handle bodily injury.

Your truck or automobile is one of your most valuable possessions, and when someone damages it, you want to make sure you recover everything that you are entitled to recover.

When someone damages your vehicle, they are required to either repair it to the condition it was in before they damaged it or to pay you the value of the vehicle. In addition, they are required to pay you for the "loss of use" of the vehicle during the time you were without your vehicle.

Your property claim will be assigned to an insurance property adjuster. If your vehicle was towed from the scene, the tow truck driver most likely took the vehicle to a storage lot. The fees paid by the storage lot get pretty high pretty quickly, so don't be surprised if the insurance company asks you to have the vehicle released within a few days. When the vehicle is released, all you are doing is agreeing to allow the vehicle be moved to a less expensive storage lot. I always think it's a good idea to agree to release your vehicle because you don't want to be in a position where you accrue storage fees that the insurance company refuses to pay. If that happens, it can get a little confusing and you could be in a fight between the storage lot and the insurance company, and its usually a fight that you don't want to have.

The insurance adjuster will ask to inspect your vehicle to prepare an estimate of the cost to repair the vehicle. This initial estimate is not exact. Many times additional damage to the vehicle will be identified after the vehicle is in for repair. If the vehicle is being repaired and the body shop finds additional damage, they will contact the insurance and get a "supplement" which will authorize the body ship to make all the necessary repairs.

If the initial estimate of the cost of repairs is high enough relative to the cost of replacing the vehicle, the insurance company may determine that your vehicle is a total loss. Many people refer to this as "totaling the vehicle". The insurance company is simply doing whatever will be less expensive.

If the vehicle is determined to be a total loss, they will not pay to repair the vehicle, they will only pay the value of the vehicle. The "total loss" amount will be two figures. One figure will be if they take possession of the wrecked car and the other is if you keep the wrecked car.

Why would you want the wrecked car? Because you can get paid for the value of the car and choose to repair it yourself. And you don't even have to repair it. Or you could get paid for the total loss and sell the salvage yourself.

It used to be that if your vehicle was a total loss, the insurance company did not have to pay you for loss of use, which we normally think of as getting a rental vehicle. Recently, the Texas Supreme Court issued an opinion that changed the law and now you are entitled to a rental car, legally referred to as "loss of use", whether your vehicle is being repaired or if it is a total loss.

A problem frequently occurs when people have a car that is only a few years old and it is a total loss. The value of the vehicle may be less than the amount that is owed on the vehicle. This is referred to as being "upside down". Its not a good situation because you are happily making your monthly payments and all of a sudden you have a wrecked vehicle that you can't drive. You may think the insurance company has to pay off the finance company, but that is not necessarily the case. The law only requires them to pay the value of the vehicle.

How do you get upside down in a car? Many times cars are financed over 6 years or sometime even longer. After a year or two, you may have paid very little on the principal but the value of the car has gone down 20 or 30%. The car is depreciating or losing value more quickly than you are paying it off.

When you purchase a new vehicle you can purchase "gap" insurance. Gap insurance is insurance that agrees to pay the balance of the note, even if the value of the vehicle is less than the note. Purchasing "gap" insurance is one way to protect yourself.

But what do you do if your car is wrecked and you didn't purchase "gap" insurance. There are no perfect solutions, but one is to recover the value of the vehicle and pay off the finance company as much as you can, and simply finance the difference and continue paying it. Another option is to purchase a new vehicle, and "roll" the "gap" into the purchase price of the new car. This option exists if you have decent credit.

I know it's a scary and difficult situation. It's one thing to be physically hurt. But when you are placed in a financial bind that is someone else's fault, it truly adds insult to injury. If you are ever in this situation, call me. I have dealt with this many times and can sometimes work something out.

If your vehicle is not a total loss, the insurance company will pay you the cost to repair the vehicle. But here is a secret. You don't have to repair the vehicle. If you have an older vehicle and it already has some dents and dings, you may prefer to pocket the money for the repairs and simply live with the vehicle with a few more dents in it. That's up to you.

You are also not required to have your vehicle repaired at the shop the insurance company sends you. The insurance company is required to pay you the reasonable value of the repairs, but you may be able to work out a better deal with a different repair shop. If you can do that, you can pocket that difference.

You are also entitled to recover "loss of use" even if you don't rent a car while yours is being repaired. Perhaps you have another vehicle and are able to make do with one less car for a while. If so, you can recover a little extra money than it costs you.

Don't overlook the possibility of getting paid for diminished value of your vehicle, as part of your property damage, especially if you have a newer model car that is wrecked. If you have a pretty new car and someone wrecks it, and the insurance company will only pay to make repairs and will not total the vehicle, you may be entitled to claim "diminished value". Diminished value is the difference in value of the car after it was repaired.

I can prove in an instant that diminished value is real. How? By showing you two identical cars, each with 10,000 miles. They are identical in every respect except one. One car was in a wreck and was repaired, the other car has never been wrecked. Which one do you want?

Everyone will choose the vehicle that was never wrecked.

They will only choose the other vehicle if they can pay less. Why? Because the fact that it has been in a wreck diminishes its value.

We can argue about how much the value has diminished, but no reasonable person can argue that there has not been some diminished value.

Finally – and this is as much a safety issue as anything – if you had a child in a car seat in the wreck, replace your car seat and insist that the insurance company pay for it. Once a child's car seat is involved in a wreck, it must be replaced, otherwise there is no assurance that the car seat will continue protecting the child.

There are a lot of things to consider when settling your property damage. If you have the right attorney, he will fight for you to make certain you recover everything that you are entitled to recover.

CHAPTER 5

How should you pick an attorney?

1. Find out how many years the attorney has been practicing. This is important to determine the amount of experience the attorney has. Personal injury cases can be very complex cases and because of that you want to make sure that you have an attorney who has the experience and resources necessary to properly prosecute your claim. I have been practicing law for over twenty-five years, which is the kind of experience you should want to handle your personal injury case.

2. Find out whether an attorney will actually be handling your claim, or whether you will be assigned to a paralegal or case manager. Many attorneys who claim to handle personal injury cases will assign the handling of the case to a non-lawyer, and getting an attorney on the phone to discuss your case can be to impossible. In large firms, your case may be assigned to an associate with little experience and that can be disastrous for you.

When you hire an attorney, you want an attorney handling your case not a case manager. And if you go to a firm because of its experience you don't want your case being handled by new attorney with little experience.

Some attorneys tell clients that their case is being handled by a "team approach" or that they roundtable cases. Ask yourself if you want one person to know your case and to be responsible for your case or would you prefer that no one is personally responsible.

3. Find out if your attorney handles primarily personal injury cases. Personal injury is a specialized area of law just like divorce law, real estate law bankruptcy or criminal law. The law is always changing and there is no way an attorney can remain up-to-date on every area of law. An attorney who handles almost exclusively personal injury matters is almost always a better choice than a general practitioner.

4. Find out if your lawyer actually goes to trial. Many attorneys who advertise for cases haven't been to trial in years, if at all. They may claim to be personal injury lawyers but all they

do is sign up cases and either settle them or farm them out to another attorney who will actually work on the case. When your case is moved from one firm to another it merely delays the time it will take for you to make a recovery because a new lawyer must learn all the facts about your case. When you hire an attorney to handle your personal injury case you want to make sure that the attorney your hiring has experience in trial and is actually the one who will be handling the case at trial and before the court.

Not all cases go to trial. Many are settled. The insurance companies know which attorneys will try cases and which ones will be forced to take a settlement because they won't take your case to trial.

5. Find out if the attorney is specifically board certified in personal injury trial law. In Texas, the State Bar has created the Texas Board of Legal Specialization and will convey special recognition to attorneys in different areas of law if those attorneys display special proficiency in that area of law. A very small percentage of attorneys are certified in personal injury trial law but if you have a personal injury case you want

to make certain that you are represented by an attorney who has demonstrated special proficiency. Before conveying certification in personal injury trial law an attorney must have been in practice at least five years, must have tried a certain number of cases before a jury, must receive recommendations from other attorneys and judges, and must pass a full day of testing in that area of law.

I have been Board Certified in Personal Injury Trial Law for over fifteen years. When you hire an attorney for your personal injury case - you want someone who specializes in that area of law.

6. Does the attorney take a fee on PIP?

Personal Injury Protection insurance or PIP is insurance that you may have which pays a portion of your medical expenses if you are involved in an automobile accident. This is your insurance and all that is required to recover is to fill out a few forms. Many lawyers will try to take a fee from their client simply for filling out these forms. I don't think that's right and I won't take a fee on your PIP. If you are considering hiring an attorney to handle your personal injury case, be sure and ask if he intends to take a fee for recovering your PIP. If so, I suggest you consider a different attorney

7. Will the attorney accept a contingent fee?

A contingent fee is a fee that is charged only if a recovery is made in a case. You should never hire an attorney in a personal injury case unless their fees and any expenses are contingent upon a recovery. An experienced personal injury attorney will never obligate you to pay expenses or a fee unless they are able to recover for you.

I will never charge a personal injury client a fee or make him pay expenses in his case unless you make a recovery.

8. Does your attorney promise that their fee will not be more than what you recover?

In some cases, a person who suffers serious injuries is limited in his recovery because of the amount of insurance the other party has. In many cases, after a case is settled, medical expenses must be repaid either directly to the doctors or to the health insurance companies. If an attorney takes his full fee and repays the medical expenses as required, the injured person may end up recovering less than the attorneys fee.

I don't think that's fair. And if a client would recover less than my contingent fee, I promise to reduce my fee to make sure that it is no more than what my client recovers.

CHAPTER 6

Should I Make a Claim?

Making a claim for personal injuries can be a difficult decision and no one should make a decision with which they are uncomfortable. Many people may have a valid claim for personal injuries and may decide that making a claim is not the right decision for them. Perhaps making a claim goes against someone's principles, and I can respect that decision. Others may feel that making a claim is simply trying to "take advantage of a situation". Others may be concerned that the process will be too time consuming or they may be concerned that they will not be able to afford an attorney. I know that the decision may be difficult, but for whatever it is worth, here are my thoughts.

If someone damaged something that you owned of value, for example your car, you would expect them to pay for the damage they caused. Not only should they pay the cost of the repairs, but they should also make sure they pay for repairs *to be done right*. If someone wrecks your car you want it repaired by someone who knows what he is doing and who uses the right materials to make the repairs. And you also want to make sure that once it is repaired that you no longer have any problems, that is, you want the repairs done right and you only want them done once.

But if all someone did was pay the cost of the repairs, have you been made whole? Getting your car repaired is a hassle. You have to take your car to the shop, you have to manage to get a ride there and back, and there is some period of time when you are without your car. You may have to worry about getting rides from someone. So if all someone does is pay the cost to repair your vehicle - have they really compensated you fully for your loss?

While people feel pretty universally that if someone damages their car they should pay for the repairs, some people feel differently when the damage is to their body and not just their car. For some reason they believe it's not as important to be made whole when the damage is to their body rather than to their car. Frankly, I couldn't disagree more. I think that damaging my body is a lot worse than damaging my car. And since it is only fair that someone compensate you fully and fairly if they damage your car, it stands to reason that they should also pay fully and fairly if they damage your body.

If you are injured and require medical treatment to treat your injuries, some people would argue that the person who injured you should only pay your medical expenses otherwise you would get a profit or a windfall. I don't think that makes sense because if I injure someone and only pay their medical expenses all I have done is put them in the place they were before I injured them, but I have done nothing to account for the fact that they had to endure doctor's visits, pain, and just the concern of whether or not they would heal and how long it would take them to get better. Medical expenses are not your only loss when you are injured, and a personal injury claim is about recovering ALL of your losses - it's about making you whole again.

CHAPTER 7

What Do You Do if You are in a Collision?

An automobile crash, even a "minor" crash, is traumatic and emotional. You can expect to experience a rush of adrenaline, fear, and confusion, among many other emotions. You were very likely on your way to meet someone, whether for an appointment, to go to work or simply on your way home. In any event, someone is probably waiting on you, and your arrival will be delayed.

The first thing you need to do is make sure you are "okay", although "okay" is a relative term. "Okay" doesn't necessarily mean you are not hurt, it only means that you are "okay". I recall someone who was badly injured when he was crossing the street. Another car hit him while it was turning left. He was thrown into the air and his head hit the windshield of the car so hard that he broke the windshield. He had several broken teeth, a fractured jaw and a broken knee. His wife, who was also hit, asked "Are you okay?", and he answered "Yes". Once you have determined that you are "okay" I suggest the following:

1. If you can, try and contact someone.

Your first thought will likely be to notify the person who is waiting on you to let them know what happened. That is a natural instinct. It is not a bad idea to contact someone and have them come to the scene. You will be upset, your mind may be racing and you want to make certain that everything that needs to be done is being taken care of.

2. Call the police

If either car cannot be driven it is especially important to call the police. They will make sure that the scene of the accident is safe and that traffic is being properly diverted. Because so many people carry cell phones, it is possible that others will have notified the police, but it is better to err on the side of caution. The police will usually notify other emergency personnel, specifically EMT's.

3. Exchange information with the other driver

Once you feel that it is safe to leave your vehicle, you should get your insurance information and driver's license and exchange information with the other driver. Be certain to write down the name, address, and driver's license number of the other driver and their insurance information. If you have a cell phone which can take pictures, it's a good idea to snap a picture of the insurance card and driver's license of the other driver in addition to taking down the information. You should also take a photograph of the license plate of the other vehicle. When taking down the insurance information, be sure and get the name of the insurance company, the policy number and the phone number of the claims office. The insurance card may also have the name of the agent who wrote the policy. When deciding what information to keep, the more information you have the better.

4. Talk to the other driver

If you can safely leave your car and speak with the other driver, make certain they are "okay" and speak with them briefly about what they recall happened. Very often they will be honest and admit that the collision was their fault. If they do, and if you are able to do so, write down what they recall happened, such as "I (the other driver) ran a red light" and have them sign the statement. The police don't come to every accident scene and getting the other driver to admit fault **and sign that statement** is especially important if the police do not come to the scene. You would be surprised at how frequently people "misremember" things once they have left the scene of the accident.

My daughter was driving in a parking lot about to exit and was stopped behind a car. The other car backed up and put a nice dent in her fender. At the scene he admitted fault and agreed to pay for the damage, but once he got home, his insurance company convinced him that he was backing very safely, making certain to look in all his mirrors and turn his head when backing, when my daughter, all of a sudden, pulled out from nowhere. The insurance company even had him say that there was nothing he could have done to be more careful backing up his car. I'm almost surprised he didn't make up a story that his wife had gotten out of his car to direct traffic with a safety vest and flags.

You don't want to be in a position where the other driver gets home and "remembers" things differently. If you can get a statement from the other driver, do it.

5.   Photograph the scene

If you are able to safely leave your vehicle, take photographs of the vehicles and of the scene of the collision with your cellphone. If you have contacted someone who arrives at the scene rather quickly, have them take photographs as well. Remember this rule - it is far better to have information and not need it, rather than to need information and not have it.

6.   Speak to witnesses

If anyone witnessed the collision, talk to them about what they saw and then take down their name, address and telephone number. If it is possible, try and document what they recall seeing or hearing and have them sign a statement. It is especially important for a witness to state which car was at fault. Collisions take place in a split second and people can see different things, so every witness may not agree on exactly what they saw. It may take an hour or more for police to arrive, and witnesses may be unable to stay and wait for the police. If a witness is not at the scene when the police arrive, it is very unlikely that the police will include that witness on the report.

7.   Talk to the police

If the police come to the scene - and in some cities, police may not arrive if the vehicles can be driven - the police officer will want your insurance card and your driver's license. They will then ask for your version of what occurred. Be certain to tell the police what happened. Be sure to tell the police if you are hurt or if you think you may be injured. If you are "shaken up" but don't feel any immediate pain, at least tell the police that you MAY be injured, rather than telling them that you were NOT injured. Not only will your adrenaline likely be high and masking pain, but some injuries start out by simply feeling "strange", but the next day or even the day after will be very painful. Be honest and also be as clear as possible when explaining what occurred to the police. It may take an hour or more for police to arrive, depending upon the time of day. If you have taken the name of a witness, be certain to give that name to the police.

Please keep in mind that officers are not perfect and sometimes make mistakes when writing their reports. The best way to make certain the police report is accurate is to be as clear as possible when explaining to the police what took place.

The police officer will usually provide you a copy of the insurance information and the name of the other driver. He should also give you the number of the police report. Be aware that it may take up to two weeks before a copy of the police report is available.

8.   Be checked by the Paramedics

Even in relatively minor collisions there are huge forces being applied. Imagine how hard you have to hit a car to cause a large dent, or to bend a bumper down, and that is how much force is being transmitted. A football player running at full speed may not cause a dent in an automobile, so you can imagine how hard you were hit if there is obvious damage to your vehicle. Those forces are being applied to the vehicle and ultimately to you. Your body is being thrown around in different directions and muscles can easily be stretched and torn. In more serious collisions you may have cuts or open wounds; and in even more serious collisions people suffer broken bones.

Regardless of the severity of the collision, it is always a good idea to be checked by the paramedics who usually arrive at the scene. Be patient with them and explain what hurts and even what feels "funny". It is not uncommon to have a strange feeling in your neck or back following collisions. You, or they, may feel that it is best that you seek immediate medical attention and even that you be transported by ambulance to the hospital. It is always best to err on the side of caution.

In one case I had, a woman refused to go by ambulance and went to the hospital on her own, only to discover that she had fractured vertebrae in her neck. Fortunately, she arrived at the hospital without incident, but imagine if she had been in even a small collision on the way to the hospital. She could have been paralyzed and her life would have been permanently changed. Paramedics take extra precaution "just in case", and while it may be uncomfortable to be placed in a cervical collar and strapped to a gurney, remember that they are doing it for your own good.

9. Talk to the tow truck driver

If your car is not able to be driven it will have to be towed from the scene. The tow truck driver may take your car to a storage yard and will provide you information to contact the storage yard to allow you to retrieve any possession or items that remained in your vehicle. Even if you are alone and transported to the hospital by ambulance, you will likely be given information about the collision, the other driver and where your vehicle has been taken.

10. Be prepared to feel sore the next day

Many times injuries that you sustained in an auto accident do not become apparent until a day or two after the collision. Even if you are treated and released by an emergency room, that does not mean you were not injured in the accident nor does it mean that you won't be in pain and discomfort following the accident. Emergency rooms don't really treat injuries. Their main goal is to make sure you are medically stabile and able to go see a regular doctor in a day or two for treatment, and if not, to admit you into the hospital for immediate treatment.

It is very common for people to suffer muscle strains and sprains in automobile accidents. These types of injuries become most apparent a day or two following the accident. People have experienced similar things when they exert themselves after not exercising for a long period of time. After they finished the activity they may be tired, but it is the next day when they really feel the effects of what they have done because muscle swelling and strain is not something that occurs immediately but usually takes a couple of days to really develop.

It is not uncommon for people who have been in auto accidents to have difficulty getting comfortable to sleep or to feel very stiff and sore, especially in the morning as well as later in the day.

CHAPTER 8

Common Injuries from Auto Collisions

Motor vehicle collision are a major cause of traumatic injuries. Injuries range from bumps and bruises, to broken bones or even death. Simply because the majority of injuries sustained in a motor vehicle collision do not result in broken bones does not mean that these injuries are not serious, nor does it mean that these injuries should not be treated. Strained muscles, whiplash and other so called "minor" injuries, can be life changing to the injured party, even if only temporarily. Sleep disruption and difficulty going about your day-to-day activities are common results of motor vehicle injuries. These interruptions are significant because it affects your ability to enjoy life. Moreover, depending upon many factors, these nagging injuries can be very slow healing and can result in long-term discomfort.

Insurance companies like to discount these injuries by referring to them as "soft tissue" injuries, but soft tissue does not mean minor, it only means that the injury did not result in a broken bone. Soft tissue injuries can not only be serious, but many times they require surgery. Most injuries sustained by professional athletes are "soft tissue" injuries, meaning there is no broken bones, yet those injuries are serious enough that to sideline professional athletes who earn tens of thousands if not hundreds of thousands of dollars each week. Nevertheless, insurance companies will argue that your injury is not serious if it is "only" soft tissue. And it is likely that when you are injured you are not in the peak of your physical shape, as athletes are.

Most soft tissue injuries, that is, injuries that do not include a broken bone, will first be treated by **physical therapy.** Physical therapy is the science of blending physiology with exercises and applying these principles to the body when an injury is sustained. Physical therapy for back and neck conditions focuses on the structures that support the spine and its joints including muscles, tendons, and ligaments. Physical therapy includes different exercises and massages that are intended to heal your muscles, ligaments and tendons.

There are five main goals of physical therapy, as described below:

1. To educate patients on the principles of stretching and strengthening, which will in turn, help manage pain and accelerate tissue healing.

2. To educate patients on proper posture and ergonomic principles to preserve the spine.

3. To accelerate the stages of healing, which focus on reducing pain and the

inflammatory cycle by applying passive modalities and perhaps ice, heat. ultrasound. traction/electrical stimulation. Healing the injury will also require introducing specific stretching exercises and progressions to abolish pain and stiffness to specific regions with high frequency and repetitions

4. To prevent future occurrences by teaching you what program is needed to deter relapses.

5. To manage exacerbations. No matter how diligent you are, you are bound to have a forgetful moment, do an activity improperly and so suffer flare ups, but new knowledge will help eliminate symptoms in a couple days, instead of suffering for weeks or months.

If your pain continues even after weeks of physical therapy, your physician may request further diagnostic studies to determine whether there may be an injury that will not respond to physical therapy. Common diagnostic tests include MRI or magnetic resonance imaging or CT scans.

Magnetic resonance imaging (MRI) is a technique that uses a magnetic field and radio waves to create detailed images of the organs and tissues within your body.

Most MRI machines are large, tube-shaped magnets. When you lie inside an MRI machine, the magnetic field temporarily realigns hydrogen atoms in your body. Radio waves cause these aligned atoms to produce very faint signals, which are used to create cross-sectional MRI images — like slices in a loaf of bread. The MRI machine can also be used to produce 3-D images that may be viewed from many different angles. MRI is a noninvasive way for your doctor to examine your organs, tissues and skeletal system. It produces high-resolution images that help diagnose a variety of problems.

Just like an X-ray allows the physician to see bone structures and determine if a bone is broken, and MRI or CT scan allows the physician to see the non-bony structures – ligaments, disc, cartridge, etc., and determine if there are any problems.

MRI of bone and joints

MRI may be used to help evaluate:

- Joint disorders, such as arthritis
- Joint abnormalities caused by traumatic or repetitive injuries
- Disk abnormalities in the spine
- Bone infections
- Tumors of the bones and soft tissues

If you continue suffering from pain even after weeks of physical therapy, your physician may suggest that you receive injections.

Injections are common in the treatment of injuries involving joint pain including back pain. They are typically considered as an option to treat joint or back pain after a course of medications and/or physical therapy is completed, but before surgery is considered. Injections can be useful both for providing pain relief and as a diagnostic tool to help identify the source of the patient's back pain.

For pain relief, injections can be more effective than an oral medication because they deliver medication directly to the anatomic location that is generating the pain. Typically, a steroid medication is injected to deliver a powerful anti-inflammatory solution directly to the area that is the source of pain. Depending on the type of injection, some forms of joint pain relief may be long lasting and some may be only temporary.

Several years ago I had pain in my thumb joint that resulted from just overuse. But it hurt every time I tried grasping something like a doorknob or opening a jar. Once it got to the point that it impacted my daily activity, my physician recommended that I get a cortisone shot. Although the shot was a little uncomfortable, after a few days my hand felt great! It's been years and I have been fine since.

Back injuries are a common injury in accidents and often times you will hear someone complain of a "herniated disc".

Your spine is made up of many different bones, called vertebrae, sitting one on top of the other. This structure allows us to bend our backs and twist in different directions. Additionally, the spine protects the spinal cord which is a large mass of nerves that travel from our brain through our spine to every part of our body.

If a bone was sitting directly on another bone, it would be painful, so our spines have a spongy substance, called a disc, between each vertebrae. These discs act as shock absorbers between the different vertebrae. We refer to the upper part of the spine as the cervical area, the middle part of the spine as the thoracic area and the lower back as the lumbar.

Occasionally, the discs can wear out and begin to protrude. Many times a disc will protrude as the result of some type of trauma to the body. This is referred to as a bulging or herniated disc, and often times this can be very painful.

Sometimes the disc bulges or herniates so much that it starts to rub against one of the nerves in the spinal cord. If the spinal canal is small, even a small disc herniation may pinch a nerve root. If the canal is large, even a sizable disc herniation may not cause any symptoms.

As stated earlier, the nerves in your spinal cord branch off to different areas of your body. If you suffer from a disc herniation, you may feel pain in your arms or legs, even though the injury is in your back. The reason this may occur is because the disc could be irritating a nerve that is traveling to your arms or legs. Generally, nerves that exit the spine in the cervical region or your neck travel down your arms while nerves that exit in the lumbar region travel to your legs and feet.

It is not uncommon for people who have a neck injury to feel pain, tingling or numbness in their arms. Likewise, people who have a lumbar injury may also feel pain, tingling or numbness in their legs.

Many injuries will resolve with physical therapy and a few require injections. Unfortunately, some injuries will not resolve even with those treatments and may require surgery. Back surgery can be a scary thing. Fortunately, doctors who perform back surgery are extremely skilled and will only recommend surgery if they believe it will resolve your pain and allow you to return to normal activities.

CHAPTER 9

Understanding Automobile insurance

Automobile insurance is often misunderstood. The industry uses terms that can be a mystery to the common person. Very often people will tell me that they have "full coverage", but this term really has no specific meaning. In reality, every insurance policy contains a bundle of different types of insurance, each covering a different loss. The type of insurance you choose to purchase is important to make certain that the losses you intend to cover, are covered. At the same time you shouldn't be purchasing insurance that you will not likely need. This chapter is intended to uncover the mystery of automobile insurance and help you make a better and more informed decision. Keep in mind, however, that each person may have unique insurance needs and that general recommendations may not necessarily apply to your situation.

Liability insurance

The most basic insurance is liability insurance and this is the coverage that is mandated by Texas law. Every automobile must be covered by the state minimum insurance which is referred to as "30/60/25".

Liability insurance covers a loss to a third person that the driver of a vehicle would be responsible to pay. In simple terms if someone causes a collision, their liability coverage will make sure the damage to the other person's vehicle is paid and that the other person's personal injury damages are covered. In essence, the liability insurance company steps into the shoes of the person who caused the wreck and pays whatever damages the responsible person should have to pay.

In personal liability automobile insurance policies, there is no deductible. The insurance company will pay the full amount you are obligated to pay to the other side up to the amount of your coverage. So long as your insurance limits are sufficient, you will not have to come out-of-pocket.

The numbers which are listed above (30/60/25) are important because they indicate the maximum amount of insurance that is available to pay damages. The first number is the number in thousands of the most money that would be paid to any one person for bodily injury; in this instance it would be $30,000. If someone is involved in the collision and the responsible party has 30/60/25 insurance coverage, the most money that can be recovered by any one person for their injuries from the responsible person is $30,000, regardless of the extent of his injuries. In many cases this is sufficient but in accidents involving serious injuries the injured party may be entitled to receive more than $30,000. Nevertheless, the most that someone can expect to recover is the maximum amount of insurance coverage maintained by the person who cased the wreck.

The second number, in this case 60, represents the total amount of money the insurance company is responsible to pay in any one occurrence for bodily injury. In this case, that means that the insurance company would not have to pay more than $60,000 regardless of how many people are injured in a collision. If there are only two people injured in a collision, the maximum amount is not important since each person could only recover $30,000 the most the insurance company would be liable for would be $60,000. However, in instances when there are more than two people involved in a collision the total amount of insurance coverage is all the insurance company is responsible of pay, regardless of the extent of injuries. For example, if there are four people injured in a collision, the insurance company for the person responsible for the wreck will pay out, at most, $60,000, regardless of how severely injured the 4 people are. If one of the injured people recovers $30,000, then the other 3 people will have to divide the remaining $30,000 among themselves. And if two people settle their claims for $30,000 each, before the other two people are able to submit their claims, the insurance company will pay nothing further since they have already paid out the maximum in the wreck for that insurance.

The final number, in this instance 25, represents the most an insurance company would have to pay for property damage caused in a collision. Today, with new cars regularly costing more than $25,000, a severe collision involving more than one other vehicle could result in someone causing more property damage than they have insurance to pay.

The amount of insurance that someone has is actually more important to the person who is been harmed than it is to the person who causes the harm. In most instances the insurance coverage is the only payment a person who is injured can realistically expect to recover. In Texas it is extremely difficult to recover money from an individual who does not have insurance coverage or does not have sufficient insurance coverage. And if someone is injured and the responsible party does not have sufficient insurance coverage, the injured person faces the possibility that he cannot recover enough money to adequately compensate him.

The minimum amount of insurance that a person must have is 30/60/25. People who request additional coverage can obtain higher amounts. Typical amounts include 50/100/30 or 100/300/50, but there is no limit to the different insurance limits that are available. The amount of liability coverage that you require depends upon your particular circumstances and it is important is that you be aware of how much insurance coverage you carry **before you need it**, because once you need insurance, it's too late to change what you have.

Uninsured/Underinsured motorist coverage

In the examples above you can easily see how it is possible that the person responsible for causing your injuries does not have sufficient insurance to properly compensate you. What happens if you are involved in a such a situation?

Fortunately, there is a way to protect yourself in the event you are injured by another person and they do not have any insurance or if they do not have enough insurance. This insurance is called ***uninsured motorist coverage*** and it is an option available to every person in Texas who has auto insurance coverage. What is important, however, is that if you want to be covered by this insurance, you have to purchase it before you need it. Once you are in a collision, if you have not purchased this coverage it is too late.

Uninsured motorist coverage is as if you are giving an insurance policy to the person who causes a collision. Uninsured motorist coverage, referred to as UM, allows you to be certain that you can recover damages if you are the victim in an automobile collision, even if the person who causes the collision has no insurance or not enough insurance. For example, let's assume that you are involved in a wreck that is not your fault and you suffer a broken leg and have $40,000 in medical expenses. The person who caused the wreck may have no insurance or may have only $30,000 in liability coverage. Assume that the fair compensation for that claim is $75,000 including all of the different factors. The person who caused the wreck may have no insurance coverage or perhaps only $30,000 in coverage, which would still leave you well short of receiving adequate compensation for your injuries. If you have purchased uninsured or underinsured motorist coverage, you can recover the difference from your own insurance. If you have $30,000 in your own uninsured or underinsured insurance coverage you can recover $30,000 from the at-fault driver's coverage (if he is insured) and an additional amount from your own underinsured motorist coverage, thereby increasing your recovery.

Another benefit of purchasing uninsured motorist coverage is that it covers you even when you are traveling in a vehicle which is not your own. If you are traveling in a friend's vehicle and he is involved in a wreck, you can utilize your uninsured motorist coverage because it not only covers you when you are in your vehicle, it covers you anytime you are involved in a motor vehicle collision. In fact, it will provide coverage for you if you are hit by a car while riding a bicycle or even walking. Insurance companies will often use the term "covered vehicle" which means the vehicles described in the insurance policy. The reason why that term is important is because many insurance coverages will protect all people riding in a "covered vehicle". The significance of this is that people will be afforded uninsured or underinsured motorist coverage so long as they are riding in a "covered vehicle". This means that everyone who is riding in your vehicle would be covered by your uninsured or underinsured motorist coverage. This is important if you are badly injured in which case you want to make certain you have all the insurance possible.

If you are riding in a vehicle that is covered by Uninsured Motorist, then you can take advantage of the UM coverage simply because you are a passenger in a "covered vehicle" even if it is not your vehicle. If you also happen to have Uninsured Motorist coverage on your own vehicle, you are considered to be an "insured person" and can take advantage of the additional insurance coverage. Of course, these situations all assume that your injuries are severe enough that you are not adequately compensated by the available liability insurance coverage.

In my opinion, uninsured motorist coverage is more important to an individual than liability coverage. Liability coverage makes sure that if you injure another person they will be able to recover money. On the other hand, if you have uninsured motorist coverage you are making certain that you will be able to recover money if someone injures you.

Secret - if you are an occupant in someone else's car when you are injured, always ask if they had Uninsured Motorist coverage. As an occupant of the vehicle, you can take advantage of that coverage if necessary.

Assume that someone is in involved in the collision and suffers bad injuries and requires surgery. The person who caused the collision has a 30/60/25 insurance policy, but the injured person has $75,000 in medical expenses, as well as lost wages and substantial pain and suffering. The most he can expect to recover from the person who caused the collision is $30,000. If the injured person has uninsured motorist coverage, not only can he recover the $30,000, but he can also recover up to the maximum amount of his uninsured motorist coverage. Not only does Texas UM coverage allow for a recovery when the other driver has no insurance, it also allows recovery when the other driver does not have enough insurance.

Insurance companies usually limit the amount of uninsured motorist coverage to the amount of your liability maximum limits. That is, if your liability limits are 30/60/25, your uninsured motorist limits are also 30/60/25. Because I think it is so important to have uninsured motorist coverage and because I want to make certain that my family is protected in the event I am severely injured in an automobile collision I have high liability limits, not necessarily to make certain I am protected if I cause a collision, but more importantly to make certain I have high uninsured motorist coverage in the event I am injured so that my family is protected.

Texas law requires an applicant for automobile insurance to sign or initial that they are rejecting UM coverage, and if the insurance company is unable to provide a signed rejection you may be able to take advantage of UM coverage if the need arises. That need would be that you are involved in a collision and the person responsible for the collision did not have insurance or did not have sufficient insurance.

Secret – If you are involved in a collision, always request the signed rejection for UM coverage. If the insurance company is unable to present the rejection, you automatically are able to take advantage of the UM coverage.

Personal Injury Protection

Personal injury protection, commonly referred to as PIP, is a no-fault coverage that covers a person's medical expenses and a portion of lost wages up to a certain amount. No-fault coverage means that the coverage is available regardless of who is at fault. What this means is that if you cause a crash, but you are injured, you can still make a claim on your PIP because it is no-fault – it doesn't matter who was at fault in causing the crash, it only matters that an injury occurred using the automobile. PIP is available to you if you have that insurance and also to everyone in a covered automobile. You can have higher PIP limits but if PIP is available, the lowest amount, and the most common amount, is $2,500.

PIP is similar to UM in that every occupant of the covered vehicle is covered. Therefore, if you are an occupant in someone else's vehicle, and they have PIP, you can collect PIP. Moreover, if you have a separate insurance coverage which has PIP, you can recover your own PIP as well.

Even though PIP only covers medical expenses and a portion of your lost wages, it is wise to pay the small additional premium for PIP, even if you have health insurance. Often you will have health insurance deductibles or co-pays which can easily add up to hundreds or even thousands of dollars, depending upon the type of health coverage you have. PIP can offset these expenses and reimburse your out-of-pocket charges.

Just as uninsured motorist coverage must be rejected by the applicant, PIP must also be rejected otherwise you will be able to take advantage of PIP coverage.

Secret - PIP is available if you are injured while occupying or around your vehicle. It does not require that you actually be in a collision. If you injure yourself, perhaps by closing the door on your hand, so long as the injury involved your automobile, you can make a PIP claim.

Medical payments

Medical payments insurance is similar to PIP except in two important aspects. It is like PIP in that it is no-fault insurance and is usually in the amount of $2,500. But it is different because unlike PIP, medical payments insurance only covers medical payments and is not cover any lost wages. Additionally, if you recover money from the responsible driver after you have made a claim on your medical payments, your insurance company may require you to repay the medical payments that were made to you. This is called "subrogation" which is the right of the insurance company to seek reimbursement. PIP does not permit the insurance company to make you pay back the money if you recover from a third party; on the other hand, medical payments coverage does allow the insurance company to make you pay them back.

Collision insurance

Collision insurance pays to repair or replace your vehicle in the event it is damaged in a collision with another vehicle or object. The state does not require a person to carry collision insurance. Collision insurance is almost always subject to a deductible, which is an initial payment amount that must be paid by the policyholder. For example, if you have a $500 deductible and your vehicle sustains damage that will cost $4000 to repair, you are responsible for the first $500 and the insurance company will pay the remainder. The higher the deductible the lower your premium will be. When determining how high your deductible should be, consider the likelihood that you may have a collision and compare how much you would be saving by increasing your deductible.

Depending upon the value of your vehicle and the cost of the collision coverage, it may not be worthwhile to even have collision coverage.

Usually, if you are still making payments on your car, the lending company requires you to have collision insurance. Why? Because the car is collateral for their loan and they want to make sure that their collateral is insured.

Comprehensive coverage

Comprehensive coverage is similar to collision coverage in that it pays for damage to your vehicle, however comprehensive coverage pays for damage to your vehicle that is not caused by a collision, usually theft, vandalism or natural causes. Comprehensive insurance usually has a deductible just as collision insurance does.

Gap Coverage

It is not unusual for a car loan to be for 60 months or even 72 months. If you have a longer term loan, the value of the car may be going down faster than your loan balance. If your car is a total loss, all that you are owed is the value of the car, regardless of how much you may owe. This could leave you in a terrible situation if you owe more on the car than it is worth.

Cars depreciate, or lose value, pretty quickly. You may purchase a new car for $20,000, and a year later that car is only worth $15,000. But if you financed the car for 5 years, you will owe more than $15,000 to the finance company. If your car is a total loss, all you can expect to receive is the car vale and you may be personally responsible for the difference to the finance company.

Fortunately, there is a type of insurance called GAP insurance which will pay the amount of the loan, regardless of what your car may be worth. The only benefit to having gap coverage is that you won't end up in a situation where your car may be a total loss, and you not have enough money to pay the finance company.

Rental car reimbursement

Rental car reimbursement ensures that you have payment for a rental car in the event your vehicle is inoperable by a covered loss.

Towing insurance

Towing insurance will pay to tell your vehicle if it is disabled.

Some people are reluctant to make a claim on their PIP or UM insurance for fear that this could increase their insurance rates. Texas law does not allow insurance companies to raise someone's rates for making one not-at-fault claim. Insurance companies do not provide insurance for free. If you have PIP or UM coverage you are almost certainly being charged for it, and no one looks forward to making a claim. You have insurance because you know that the possibility exists that you may one day be forced to make a claim.

I hope this gives you some insight on the different insurance available. If you are confused or would like to discuss this with me, give me a call. Be assured that if I am representing someone for an injury my only goal is to maximize their recovery.

Sometimes people ask me why I have such a fascination with insurance coverage and wonder whether I want auto wrecks to occur. Well, of course not. Asking that question is no different than asking if someone wants heart attacks to occur because they advocate for heart defibrillators in buildings. Those defibrillators save people's lives, but if you don't plan in advance they won't be there when you need them.

Similarly, insurance protects us financially when disaster strikes. But we have to plan in advance. My house flooded twice in less than a year and believe me when I tell you it was the last thing I wanted to happen. But I was certainly glad I had purchased flood insurance.

I want to help make sure that you have the protection you need and also want to help you in the event you are ever injured or involved in a car wreck to make sure you recover every penny to which you are entitled.

CHAPTER 10

Being Safe

There are too many collisions. Although my goal as an attorney is to make certain my clients are fairly compensated if they are injured, my hope is that people will be safe and not cause injuries in the first place. It is often said "if you have your health you have everything", unfortunately it is only when people actually lose their health that they appreciate how true that statement is.

Traffic fatalities in Texas steadily dropped until 2003 when they started to steadily increase. In 2014, more people died on Texas roadways than were lost on 9/11 and traffic fatalities have increased 20% since 2003.

Single vehicle, run-off the road crashes resulted in 1,384 deaths in 2014 which was almost 40% of all traffic fatalities. Think about that. More than 1,000 people died in a single vehicle crash which were likely completely preventable. Fatalities in rural areas accounted for 55% of all fatalities.

Intersectional collisions resulted in almost 25% of all fatalities and head-on collisions took the lives of 581 people. Sadly, there was not a single day in 2014, nor in most years, when there is not at least one traffic fatality in the State of Texas.

One of the most important things someone can do to avoid a serious injury or death, is to use proper restraints. Passengers should always use a seatbelt and small children should be placed in a proper car seat. In 2014, 43.8% of all traffic fatalities reported that improper restraints were used.

Alcohol and drugs is also a significant factor contributing to violent collisions. Over 1,000 traffic deaths involved a driver who was under the influence of drugs or alcohol. And most crashes involving a DUI occur between 10 p.m. and 3 a.m., with the most likely time being between 2 and 3 a.m. Not surprisingly, the most dangerous time to be on the road is Saturday night.

One area which is beginning to be a greater and greater concern is the "distracted driver", which is simply when the operator of a vehicle is engaged in some activity that distracts them from their primary task of driving and increases their risk of an accident. There are four types of distractions that can cause a driver to be distracted and increase the chance of an accident. These include the following:

Visual - looking at something other than the roadway

Auditory - hearing something that is not related to driving

Manual - manipulating something other than the steering wheel

Cognitive - thinking about something other than driving.

Any distraction potentially endangers the driver, passengers and bystanders and some activities can cause multiple types of distractions which makes these activities even more dangerous. For example, if you are looking at a map while driving there is a visual distraction – you are looking at something other than the road – there is a manual distraction – you are holding something other than the steering wheel and there is a cognitive distraction – your mind is being taken off driving.

Distractions can be inside the car, such as the radio, looking at maps, or simply people talking. They may also be external such as roadside signs, rubber necking at a collision site or scenery.

Years ago the most common distraction was the car radio. Many people have been seriously injured because the driver has been distracted either listening to the radio which might cause his mind to wander and to not pay attention to outside dangers, or the driver may be changing the station or volume which diverts his eyes from the road.

Without question the most dangerous recent phenomena which has been the source of driver distraction is the cell phone and particularly texting. The simple act of texting while driving is a visual, cognitive, and manual distraction that has significantly increased the number of automobile accidents.

Texting has become a common source of communication. A study done in December

2012 showed that 170 billion text messages were sent in the United States. Modern technology has enabled us to literally stay in constant contact with one another. All too often, we feel the urge to maintain this contact even when operating our vehicles, often while traveling at high rates of speed.

The average driver who texts while driving takes his eyes off the road for five seconds. If one is traveling at 55 mph that would be like driving the length of a football field with your eyes closed. One study found that texting, browsing and dialing a smart phone is now the most distracting activity engaged in by drivers. The simple activity of making phone calls while driving - including reaching for the phone, looking up numbers and dialing - tripled the risk of an automobile crash. Other studies have found that the risk of a crash while using a phone is even greater.

Most distressing is the reality that the younger the driver, the more likely they are to be using a smart phone while driving. This means that the younger, less experienced driver is the one who is most likely to be engaging in an activity that is causing him to be significantly distracted while driving.

You may ask yourself what the alternative may be. Am I suggesting that you not look at a map while driving? Or that you not text while driving? The answer is "Yes". Resist the urge.

It can happen to anyone and it can happen in an instant. A friend of mine was driving with his family when another driver was distracted and came into his lane of traffic. My friend and his wife died instantly and two of his children have permanent, life changing injuries. The driver of the other vehicle lost his wife in the collision. And the distraction? He was trying to locate a DVD to play for his child. I know it sounds extreme to pull off the road before looking for directions on your phone or sending that text, but either ask your passenger to do it for you or if you are alone, pull over. If you are on a long drive you could probably use the break.

The bottom line is this. Your chances of getting into an accident are far greater when you are engaging in dangerous activities. Don't drink and drive. Don't text and drive. Stay safe.

CHAPTER 11

What Can I Expect if I Make a Claim?

Making a claim for injuries is not a simple process. There are two parts of a claim: liability and damages. Liability is establishing who was at fault. Damages are determining how much the person has lost as a result of the accident.

Liability is established through the police records, witness statements, and photographs of the vehicles and the collision site. Many times liability is easily established, however it can never be taken for granted. If you are not able to prove the other person caused the accident you are not able to recover damages. Therefore, even if liability is apparently clear, steps should be taken to make certain that liability facts are preserved otherwise the insurance company may try to deny paying a claim.

In injury claims damages include **medical expenses, physical pain and mental anguish, impairment, disfigurement**, and **lost wages**.

Medical expenses incurred in the past are proven by obtaining copies of the medical bills.

Future medical expenses can be proven through written statements from medical professionals indicating their estimate of the medical treatment that will be required in the future and the cost of that treatment.

Loss of income can be an important part of the damages in a claim. Usually the human resources department of an employer will furnish a statement indicating the amount of work lost and the wages that would have been earned. Many people ask if they are able to recover lost wages if they did not miss any pay because they had sick leave or vacation leave to use for their time missed from work due to their injury.

Even if you did not miss any pay but had to use your sick leave or vacation leave for time missed from work you are entitled to recover the amount of wages you would have earned. The reason is because your sick time and vacation time has a value to you and if you had to use that accrued time because you are recuperating from an injury you are entitled to recover the value of that time which is the same as your wages.

Medical expenses and lost income are not too difficult to quantify. That is, even though there may be a disagreement about what is reasonable and necessary, there is a mathematical formula to determine these amounts. Some people refer to these damages as "economic loss" because they cause a direct economic loss to the victim. In addition to medical expenses and lost income, an injured person is entitled to three categories of damages which are not so easy to quantify. These damages are (1) physical pain and mental anguish, (2) physical impairment and (3) physical disfigurement.

Physical pain and mental anguish is compensation for the actual pain someone was caused while mental anguish in the anxiety, worry and stress that resulted from the injury. Anyone who has been in pain knows what that is and that it is real. Mental anguish is something which is no less real, but may be something which you have not considered. When you suffer an injury there is anxiety and concern associated with that injury. Some of the concern is whether you will ever feel better. You may have anxiety about how you will care for your family if you are injured or unable to work. You may experience fear when confronted with a similar circumstance. For example, it is common for people who have been involved in a car wreck to be afraid to drive or they may suffer nightmares. All of these factors contribute to determining fair compensation for physical pain and mental anguish.

Physical disfigurement is compensation for any disfigurement that resulted from an injury. The most common type of disfigurement would be scarring but also includes a loss of limb. Fair compensation for physical disfigurement depends on the severity of the scarring and where that scarring is located. For example, a scar on someone's back would be considered less than a scar that was always visible, such as a scar on someone's face. Obviously, the more severe the scarring or disfigurement, the greater the compensation one would expect to recover.

Physical impairment is the final element of damage to be considered. Impairment is simply compensation for being unable to do certain things that you were once able to do before being injured. Determining appropriate compensation for impairment depends upon being able to describe the activities that someone is prevented from participating in, the length of time one is unable to engage in those activities and how important those activities had been. For example, if someone injured their back and was unable to play golf that limitation would be considered an element of physical impairment. The degree of impairment would be greater to someone who played golf several times a week rather than to someone who played once per month.

When discussing your claim with an attorney it is important that he discuss all of these elements with you, especially the three "non-economic" types of damages, otherwise he will not be able to fully and fairly evaluate the damages you have sustained.

In claims that are less complicated, the insurance company may accept liability for their insured if the liability facts are properly documented and given to the insurance company. In those instances, claims may be settled once all of the medical documentation proving the extent of the injury as well as lost wages is presented to the insurance company. In certain claims, it may be advantageous to the injured party if an agreed settlement can be made because it can usually be done relatively quickly.

Often no agreement can be reached with the insurance company and claims cannot be settled without filing a lawsuit.

A lawsuit begins by filing an original petition in court. The injured person is called the plaintiff in the lawsuit and the person responsible for causing the collision is referred to as the defendant. Once a lawsuit is filed, the defendant is actually handed a copy of the lawsuit by a process server. This is called "being served with a lawsuit".

After a defendant is served, he will usually present a copy of the lawsuit to his insurance company who will retain an attorney to defend him in the suit. Once an attorney has been retained for the defendant, that attorney will file an answer in court. Typically, the answer is very simple and simply denies the facts that are alleged in the Original Petition.

Once an answer is filed by the defendant, the plaintiff's attorney becomes aware of the attorney representing the defendant and these attorneys will communicate for the remainder of the case. The plaintiff and the defendant will usually exchange discovery. Discovery is how each side learns the facts that the other side will try to prove. Since the plaintiff is the one who is trying to prove his case, it is usually most important for the plaintiff to provide full and complete discovery to the defendant setting forth all of his injuries and damages.

Discovery usually includes written questions directed to the plaintiff as well as written requests for certain documents. The written questions, called interrogatories, ask specific details about the facts of the collision, about the injured person, and the injuries he sustained. The defendant will usually want a medical history including information about any prior injuries or lawsuits that the plaintiff has had. The defendant will ask for documents relating to the injuries and the vehicle damage.

Once the two sides exchange written discovery and responses, it is common for the deposition of the plaintiff and the defendant to be taken. The deposition is the one and only chance that I have to directly question the defendant in person. It also represents the only chance that the defendant has to question the injured person. A deposition usually takes place in the conference room and everything said in the room is recorded by a court reporter. Many times the only people present at the deposition are the attorneys, the witness and the court reporter. There is no judge present at a deposition. The lawyer asks the witness questions, and the witness (which may be you) responds. The court reporter takes down every word that is said and after the deposition, presents the testimony in a booklet form to the attorneys.

Depositions usually begin with the attorney asking basic questions like where you live, are you married and what you do for a living. They also ask questions about what happened and what your injuries were.

Once the deposition is concluded the court reporter will type up a transcript of what was said in the deposition. The transcript will be in a question and answer format. Before the deposition takes place the witness swears to tell the truth, and when you give your deposition it is very important that everything you say is truthful.

In some cases, where there are additional witnesses, their deposition may be taken as well.

The discovery process may take 9 to 12 months and in some cases even longer.

At some point in the litigation, after the parties believe that they have enough information to evaluate their claim, it is common for the parties to mediate their claims. Mediation is a formal attempt by the parties to settle their client. The mediator is a neutral party whose only responsibility is to get each party to compromise enough to reach a settlement agreement. Mediation usually takes place in the office of the mediator.

The mediation usually begins with all parties seated around a large conference table. After the mediator introduces himself and explains the mediation process the plaintiff, through his attorney, will spend a few minutes talking about his case and explaining the liability and damages. The defense attorney will then present their defense and explain why they believe the damages are not as large as the plaintiff claims. Once the two parties discuss their case together they are usually taken to separate rooms. From that point on the mediator goes back and forth between the two rooms talking with each party about the strengths and weaknesses of his case and trying to get the parties to reach an agreement.

If mediation is successful, the parties will reach an agreement and the case will conclude.

If the parties cannot reach an agreement, the case will proceed to trial. Getting your case to trial can be frustrating. There are many more cases than there are courts and every case must wait its turn before it can be reached for trial

When a case is set for trial for a particular date the case may be tried any time within two weeks of that date. More times than not when a case is set for trial it will not be called within that two-week period and the trial date will be reset.

Trials can be stressful. A tremendous amount of preparation goes into every trial. Trials can last anywhere from just a few days to a few weeks. Complicated cases have been known to last for many months. The most important part of a trial is presenting witnesses who testify before the jury and presenting evidence, like photographs, medical records and other documents, to the jury. Once the plaintiff and defendant put on their case, the jury is told to deliberate and reach a decision.

The jury decides the case by answering specific questions that are given to them by the court in what is called a "jury charge". The questions do not specifically ask who should win and sometimes the jury is not aware of the effect of their answers to these questions. Once the jury has reached its decision, the jury's verdict is read.

Although trials can be exciting it can be very difficult to have one's fate in the hands of 12 strangers. For this reason, it is often preferable for the two sides to reach an agreement and settle their differences rather than have the decision made by a jury of strangers.

CHAPTER 12

Frequently asked questions?

1. How long does it take to finish my case?

There are too many variables in a case to predict how long it may take to settle your claim. Every case is different. If everything goes smoothly, it's possible to conclude a rather straightforward automobile case with relatively minor injuries that resolve in 6 to 8 weeks, in about 6 months from the date of the injury. But that is if everything goes smoothly.

2. What can happen that can cause delays in settling a claim.

If your injuries take longer to resolve than expected, settlement of your case can take longer. It is very important that the full picture of your injuries be considered when settling your case. It may take time to determine if your injuries have resolved and what additional treatment you may need. Other factors that can delay resolution of your claim can be difficulty in obtaining medical and billing records, delays in receiving information from your employer about lost wages, or simply that insurance adjusters are overworked and can't get to your particular claim.

My goal as your attorney is to resolve your claim as quickly as possible but at the same time making sure I recover everything to which you are entitled.

3. If my car requires repair, do I get a rental car?

If your vehicle is damaged and is able to be repaired, the person causing the damage is required to pay to repair your vehicle as well as provide a replacement vehicle for you to use while your car is being repaired.

4. Does the insurance company give me enough money to rent a car?

Insurance companies will usually only allow $25 or $30 per day for a vehicle rental. Fortunately, many rental car companies have what they refer to as an "insurance rate" which is a discount to people who are renting a vehicle through an insurance company. The discounted rate allows you to get a vehicle for the amount that the insurance company authorizes.

5. What happens if the repair shop discovers additional damage once they begin repairs?

Its pretty common for the cost of repairs to increase once repairs begin. The original estimate is made before any of the body parts are removed and body shops often discover additional damage. They will contact the insurance company and get what is referred to as a supplement to make sure the repairs can proceed.

6. The insurance company wants me to release my car to them from the storage yard. Should I agree to this?

If your vehicle is towed from the scene of the accident it is often taken to a storage facility.

These storage yards charge a daily rate for storage which is probably higher than most places, and these charges can add up. Many large insurance companies work together to provide vehicle storage at a more affordable rate and will request that your vehicle be moved to one of their lots. There is no reason not to agree to this and if you don't, there is a possibility that you could be stuck with the high storage fees. You are not giving up any rights by allowing the insurance company to move your vehicle. You are simply cutting down some of the expenses the insurance company will incur. The problem for you is that if the insurance company spends too much on storage fees, they may negotiate harder on parts of the claim that could benefit you, like your injury claim.

7. **What does it mean to settle a case?**

A case settles if, and when, you and the insurance company reach an agreement about how much to accept for the claim. If you and the insurance company can't agree on the amount to settle, the case can be tried in court and the decision will be made by the jury.

8. Will the insurance company repair or replaced while I am still getting treated for injuries?

An auto claim often involves two parts – property damage and bodily injury. The insurance company usually assigns one adjuster to handle the property damage and another who only deals with bodily injury. Even if they don't assign two adjusters, property damage is treated separately from bodily reason. This allows you to settle any property damage separate from any claim for bodily injury. Just because you settle your property damage claim doesn't mean that you have settled your bodily injury claim.

9. What does it mean to file suit?

In most instances, we will present our estimate of damages to the insurance company to determine if a settlement can be reached. Sometimes, we are able to reach an agreement rather easily and the claim is resolved. In other instances, we can't reach an agreement. If the parties can't reach an agreement, we may file suit. Filing suit means that we file papers with the court starting an actual lawsuit, rather than simply presenting a claim to the insurance company.

10. Is suit filed against the insurance company?

Even though I am almost always dealing directly with the driver's insurance company rather than directly with the drover, if suit is filed, suit is filed against the person who caused the wreck, not against his insurance company. In some states you can file suit against the insurance company, but in Texas you file suit against the person who caused the wreck. However, the insurance company will appoint and pay for an attorney to represent the person.

11. If a lawsuit is filed, does that mean my case won't settle?

No. It is not unusual to file suit in a case but even after suit is filed, the majority of cases settle without having to go to trial.

12. Do I have to finish my case in two years?

In Texas, as in most states, there is a "statute of limitations" which is a time period in which you must bring suit. Most injury claims in Texas have a two year statute of limitations. This only means that a lawsuit must be filed within two years of the date of injury; it does not mean that the case must be finished within two years. If you don't file a lawsuit within two years of the date of injury, it may be difficult, if not impossible, to seek any recovery for those injuries.

As your attorney, I carefully monitor your case to make certain all deadlines are met.

13. What is the use of filing a lawsuit if the case is going to settle anyway?

There are many reasons why it may be necessary to file suit on a case. Insurance companies assign an adjuster to evaluate claims. Sometimes, an adjuster makes an opinion about the value of a claim and his opinion won't budge. Once suit is filed in a case the claim is reassigned to a different adjuster who may form a different opinion about the value of the claim.

Another reason to file suit is because once a suit is filed we have access to information that may not be available before suit is filed. Once a suit is filed we come under the jurisdiction of the court, and the court can require the other side to disclose information that wasn't otherwise available. Prior to filing suit, I usually provide information to the other side to assist them in evaluating the case, and sometimes the other side cooperates. But the other side has no obligation to provide information until a suit is filed. One important piece of information is the policy limits available and mots insurance companies won't disclose this until a lawsuit is filed.

14. If my health expenses were paid by my health insurance, do I need to pay my health insurance back?

Usually. One of the elements of damages which you can recover is medical expenses. If the medical expenses are paid by your health insurance company, your health insurance can claim what is called "subrogation" which means that the health insurance company gets paid back if you make a recovery. As your attorney, one of the things I do is try to make sure every party that is claiming payment – especially medical providers – are repaid so that you don't have to worry about it.

15. If I settle my case and later discover that I need more medical care, can I get any more money?

No. When we evaluate your claim we consider both past and future medical expenses. In many instances you fully recover before we finish your case, but sometimes your medical problems can take years to resolve, and some may never resolve. In those instances we get a doctor to predict what your future medical problems will be and provide an estimate for the cost of treating those problems, and we use those estimates in determining a fair amount to finish your claim. But once a claim is finished; it is finished. That is why it's important that we calculate any future care carefully to make certain that all your future needs are met.

CHAPTER 13

What Should I Expect from my Attorney?

I believe that attorneys provide valuable information and guidance to people who have been injured in an automobile collision. Most importantly, the proper attorney has experience in handling automobile collision claims to make certain that you are able to obtain all of the compensation that you are entitled to.

When people ask me whether they need an attorney, I am reminded of the time my wife wanted to have a new light fixture installed in my daughter's bedroom. We went to a Big Box hardware store where she picked out a fixture. While we were there, we spoke with the salesman about the need to get an electrician. He assured us that installing the fixture was rather simple, how I will see a black wire and a white wire and how to connect them to the fixture. I listened to him intently and even took notes.

I have an MBA from one of the best graduate business schools in the country and my law degree is from one of the best law schools in the country. I figured that someone who had these kinds of degrees could follow the instructions of the guy at the hardware store. Or so I thought.

When we got home I tried to do everything like he told me to do. When I switched the power on to the house, the entire back of the house was dark. Fortunately, it only cost me $150 to have an electrician come undo whatever I had done and install the fixture properly.

What I learned was that while I may know a whole lot about certain areas of the law, and especially helping injured people, I need to stick with what I know. And what I know is how to handle injury cases.

Hopefully, you have never been involved in an automobile collision. But if you are, be assured that while it may be a unique situation to you, it is something I have handled hundreds upon hundreds of times. I am familiar with what needs to be done and how best to make sure that your claim is handled properly and thoroughly so you receive the fair compensation that you should receive.

The first thing I make sure to do is to listen to your problems and make certain that your immediate needs are addressed. You are likely without a vehicle and also in need of medical treatment. After you meet with me and I become your attorney, I try to take your problems and make them mine, so you can concentrate on getting your life back together and recovering from any injuries.

I immediately contact the insurance company and let them know that from this point forward, they are not to bother you and instead they should contact me with any questions. I will also do whatever I can to make certain you are provided a rental vehicle.

If you need medical treatment, not only will I make certain that you are receiving the care that you need, but I can also make certain that financial arrangements are made to minimize any out-of-pocket expenses you may be incurring.

In certain circumstances, an immediate investigation is appropriate to make certain the facts of the collision are well documented. This may include photographing the scene, speaking to witnesses or even engaging accident reconstruction experts. Be assured that whatever should be done in your case will be done and you will not have to pay out-of-pocket.

You may be entitled to additional payments from different sources of insurance, and I will work to make sure that the paperwork is completed to get you that coverage.

I will also begin the process of gathering all of the documents necessary to begin presenting your claim to the insurance company. These documents include all your medical bills and records as well as any documentation regarding lost time from work. Getting these records early can save time later.

You may be receiving bills or notifications of payment due from hospitals, ambulance services or doctors. I know what an irritation this can be and I contact the medical provider to let them know that you were the victim of an automobile collision and that your bill will be paid once we resolve your claim. While most medical billing companies will wait for payment, some require additional letters from me to leave you alone. I know what you are going through and how upsetting it can be to keep receiving these bills, so I will keep writing them as often as necessary to get them to stop bothering you.

If you have health insurance, I will also contact them for a few reasons. First, your health insurance may be a great resource to identify your different medical providers. Second, your health plan may require you to reimburse them. I am careful about keeping track of all of this so that once your case resolves, all of your medical bills are paid and there are no "loose ends" for you to concern yourself. Once your claim is done; I want it to be totally "DONE".

In almost every case, the other side will make a settlement offer. I keep you informed about these offers and any ongoing negotiation. While I will advise you and make recommendations on negotiations, the decision whether to settle your claim is always yours.

I also evaluate every claim carefully to determine whether a claim is appropriate for settlement without filing a lawsuit, and which claims will require a suit to be filed. When it is appropriate to file suit, that is what is done.

Whatever the case, I am always available for my clients, helping them make the best decisions on their claim and fighting to recover every dollar I can on their behalf.

If you ever have the need for an attorney, please contact me. If I can't help you, I will find someone who can. I look forward to hearing from you.

Michael R. Wadler
2100 West Loop South, Suite 1100
Houston, Texas 77027

713/979-5936
wadler@hhjwlaw.com

www.ingramcontent.com/pod-product-compliance
Lightning Source LLC
Chambersburg PA
CBHW070047210526
45170CB00012B/608